Silas Ketchum

The Original Sources of Historical Knowledge

A plea for their preservation

Silas Ketchum

The Original Sources of Historical Knowledge
A plea for their preservation

ISBN/EAN: 9783337248581

Printed in Europe, USA, Canada, Australia, Japan

Cover: Foto ©ninafisch / pixelio.de

More available books at **www.hansebooks.com**

THE

ORIGINAL SOURCES

OF

HISTORICAL

KNOWLEDGE.

A PLEA FOR THEIR PRESERVATION.

BY REV. SILAS KETCHUM,

PRESIDENT OF THE NEW HAMPSHIRE ANTIQUARIAN SOCIETY;
MEMBER OF THE HISTORICAL SOCIETIES OF
NEW HAMPSHIRE AND NEW YORK.

WINDSOR (Ct.):
(125 COPIES FOR PRIVATE DISTRIBUTION.)
George Crowell Ketchum, Printer.
1879.

With smoking axle hot with speed, with steeds of fire and steam,
Wide-waked Today leaves Yesterday behind him like a dream.
Still from the hurrying train of Life, fly backward far and fast
The milestones of the Fathers, the landmarks of the Past.

JOHN G. WHITTIER.

ORIGINAL SOURCES

OF

HISTORICAL KNOWLEDGE.

———∞◦◦◦◦———

[NOTE.— Some of the statements and illustrations, and most of
the recommendations, contained in this essay, were used in an Address by the writer before the New Hampshire Historical Society,
at its Annual Meeting in Concord, 13 June, 1877.]

———∞◦◦◦◦———

KNOWING so well as I do the destruction that has
already overtaken the historical records of the
fathers, and the calamities which have fallen on the
lares and penates of our New England homes, I desire to make a plea for their preservation.

I shall name a few of those original sources of historical knowledge which are generally the least
prized, and so most likely to be slighted and destroyed. I shall also attempt to point out a practicable method for their aggregation at a convenient
place; to indicate in outline a system for their arrangement and classification; and a method whereby
they can be made most easily accessible, and most

readily available to the enquirer after facts, and for all purposes of history or law.

JOHN FARMER has been styled "the Father of New England Genealogy." He was in a conspicuous sense the founder of the New Hampshire Historical Society, and edited the first five volumes of its collections. He laid the foundations for Savage's Genealogical Dictionary. He set the example of writing town histories. He gave currency to the project of a periodical literature devoted exclusively to American history. The New England Historic, Genealogical Society was established by his pupils.*

Under the impulse of forces which he more than any other man set in motion ; by the energy of proclivities to which he by counsel and example gave wise direction ; the boundaries of legitimate history have been much enlarged, and the subjects of historical enquiry considerably multiplied in these latter days.

States and empires, crowns and dynasties, revolutions and invasions are no longer considered the

---

* In a letter from Hon. John Wentworth, LL. D., of Chicago, he assures me his enthusiasm for genealogical pursuits was first aroused by the letters of JOHN FARMER to his father, making enquiries concerning the early members of the Wentworth family. so long distinguished in New Hampshire affairs. * How many men took the fever from the same contact it would be impossible to determine. But when we recall to mind the men who, being younger than he, were brought into intimate relations with this great Anti quary—Bouton, Drake, Towne, the sons of Jacob Bailey Moore, Jr., the Spaldings, the Bells, and many others—and then note the character of their literary labors and favorite pursuits, we cannot fail to see how this quiet, unobtrusive, patient and careful man repeated himself, without intention, in the generation which succeeded him.

* I find that MR. WENTWORTH also states the same thing, in the Preface to the WENT-WORTH GENEALOGY, 1 v. 1873

only proper subjects of record, or as presenting the only themes worthy of the true historian's ambition. For histories of churches, parishes, societies, associations, institutions, towns, cities, and even peculiar local customs, social and religious movements, secular enterprises and industries, there is already a large demand. And the delight taken in their study and preparation may be expected to increase in due proportion to the increase of intelligence and culture. These works may not reach to that high importance ascribed to the more pretentious labors of the recognized historian. Nevertheless, the accuracy, extent and variety of information, contained in the larger, are often derived from these humbler and inferior treasuries of facts.* In the days of Bradford, Morton, Hubbard and Winthrop, American history could hardly be more than a series of memoranda, detailing local events. It is only within this century that it became very generally recognized that we had any history to write.

Nor is biography—the history of a life—any longer confined to the "great ones." Many men are found to be locally great—in influence and power. No man can be the proper historian of a town or state, that does not clearly discern the influence, on

* Family tradition and genealogical history is [are] the very reverse of amber which, itself a valuable substance, usually includes flies, straws, and other trifles ; whereas these studies, being themselves insignificant and trifling, do nevertheless serve to perpetuate a great deal of what is rare and valuable in ancient manners, and to record many curious and minute facts which could have been preserved and conveyed through no other medium.—*Sir W. Scott*, "*Waverly*," ch. iv.

their character and destiny, of the opinions and example of their leading citizens. *

And in the transformation of ideas which has swept over the nation and the nations in this hundred years, the importance of the local community, like that of the single person, has been much enhanced. The love of family, which we inherit from our English ancestors; the love of one's own which is inherent in most men; and the assumed *par excellence* of every citizen, which our American individualism has pushed conspicuously into focus; have all conspired to endow with unusual interest and dignity enquiries into the traits, employments, social status and general influence of the *individual*, in every walk of life.

Moreover, Americans are beginning to feel that they have an ancestry to be proud of. To bear a name that was borne in the Mayflower is like bearing one that came in with the Conqueror. To find one's patronymic in Savage is next to finding it in Burke. And there are few families therein named (that have obeyed the command to multiply), that have not in some of their members attained an honorable distinction.

It is gratifying to observe the large and healthy increase of interest among Americans in simply family history. If it is true that those who care for their ancestors will care for their posterity, it ought to be hailed with gratitude as a cheering sign of the times.

---

* Take, for example, Benjamin Bellows in Walpole ;   Amos Shepard in Alstead ; Francis Davis in Warner ; Christopher Hussey in Hampton ; Ebenezer Webster in Salisbury ; John Hazen in Haverhill ; Jacob Bailey in Newbury and Jacob Davis in Montpelier ; the Tyngs in Old Dunstable ; Benjamin Pierce in Hillsborough ; and scores of others which might be named.

and what were his children's names. Surely, when
we examine the array of volumes devoted to family
history, which every well-furnished, historical library
now presents, we cannot be unaware of the propor-
tions to which this literary industry has grown ; nor
ought we to underrate the importance which may
possibly attach to the most *un*important facts, in the
estimation of those engaged in it, and who ought to
be competent to judge in such matters.

I. is probable that the peculiar circumstances of
our condition, as a nation of recent origin, made up
of communities some of which have been settled
"within the memory of men still living," and many
within the remembrance of their fathers, for the com-
pilation of whose history so much material is supposed to be accessible, has tended to encourage a
disregard for those Sources of historical knowledge
we are beginning to so highly prize. It doubtless
never occured to the first settlers in the forest that
they were making history ; or that the facts of their
lives, or the transactions of their public meetings
would ever become subjects of historical inquiry.
Their care to secure and preserve good titles to their
estates, and to transact all business legally, made the
early proprietors generally dilligent to keep faithful
records of their doings ; and, although in many cases
meagre and incomplete, yet they become of great
interest to the local historian. The early records of
births, marriages and deaths, and of many events of
local importance are, however, surprising for their full-
ness, when we consider the character and employments of the first settlers of our towns generally.

But, with all these helps invaluable, he who pur-
sues enquiries into local or personal history becomes

at once aware that a vast number of facts, desirable
to be known, are no where recorded in order, if at all.
It is probable that the same degree of importance
may attach to no subsequent generation, that does
attach to the first inhabitants of a town or state. Men
in the commonest walks of life, whose education,
talents or ability would never have made them conspicuous in older communities, become historic as
pioneers. They have in innumerable instances, and
in no small degree, helped to lay the foundations,
and give shape and character to the institutions, of
towns which have in turn exerted much influence on
the affairs of the state. On the other hand, many
towns were settled by men of high intelligence, good
education and unusual ability. This was particularly true of Dover, Portsmouth, Exeter, Hampton,
Charlestown, Salisbury, Hanover, Haverhill and
many others in New Hampshire. The men who
cleared the forests, subdued the soil, erected homes,
founded churches, put in operation the machinery of
local government and established permanent institutions, were men of diversity of talents, attained much
experience in affairs, accumulated great masses of
private papers which would reveal a tolerably fair
record of their lives and times; but they wrote no
history ; seldom made a memorandum designed for
a historical purpose. They were otherwise employed.
It is doubtful if they understood the magnitude and
significance of their part in the drama in which they
were actors. Nevertheless now, not a century after
they have gone to their rest, men eagerly piece together the fragmentary records of their labors, and
the story of their lives, thus constructed, reads like a
romance. Who shall say that the zeal and endeavor

to recover and preserve such facts is a fruitless toil ? "Let his name, and the name of his posterity, be blotted forever from the memory of mankind."

If, for instance, the general mass of facts preserved in Savage's Dictionary are to be considered as in any sense valuable, surely we cannot estimate as unimportant any authority which throws a gleam of certain light on the humblest individual in society. Not only does every man become the possible progenitor of a Franklin, a Webster or a Wilson ; but every man belongs to a family whose history is liable—and, according to present indications, likely— to be written. It seems to be morally certain that, at some time or other, somebody will be in quest of all there is to be known, not only concerning the commander at Bunker Hill, *clarum et venerabile nomen*,* but also concerning

"Honest John Tompkins the hedger and ditcher."

And the preservation of authentic information is the more desirable, because fable has often been accepted for fact, and has come near to usurp its place in history. The story that Henry Wilson was born in a gypsy camp was believed, and circulated as true, by well informed men, and was only finally killed, after his decease, by the testimony of family papers.†
The story of David Thomson, the first settler in New Hampshire, as told by Hubbard, accepted by Belknap, and passing current in history for more than two hundred years, is finally overthrown and the truth apparently established, by the discovery of an

* *Quid ?*— See the controversies of the Centennial year.

† Extracts from these were published in the Boston *Herald* by his uncle, Jeremiah S. Colbath, of New Durham, N. H., a few days after the Vice President's death.

indenture, among the private papers of Gov. John Winthrop, by his worthy descendant the Hon. Robert C. Winthrop, of Boston.* Whether Richard Potter, a man of New Hampshire though not a New Hampshire man, was a native of the East or West Indies, of Boston, London, or New Orleans, is a question to which no man is able to give a certain answer, and it has been gravely asserted that he was a son of Benjamin Franklin. And yet, Richard Potter lived twenty years in Massachusetts, and fifteen years in New Hampshire, both within the present century, is remembered by thousands still living, and was almost as well known in his day as Daniel Webster.†

No man has attempted to write the history of a town, or a family, or even of a single life, but he has discovered that events, of no small importance, and occurring within times not yet forgotten, cannot be established beyond a peradventure.

To illustrate : I endeavored for some years to piece together the facts in the life of a man who was an active magistrate for twenty-seven years, a man of influence in the town where he lived, was marked by physical characteristics that distinguished him from all other men (which would naturally excite the curiosity and enquiries of his townsmen), and was well known in three counties ; and I could learn neither when nor where he was born, nothing of his ancestry, nor the whereabouts of his descendants, nor when nor

---

* This Indenture, with a valuable paper thereon by Charles Dean, Esq., of Cambridge, is printed in *Proceedings* of the Massachusetts Historical Society, 1875—76.

† In 1876 I collected all the facts I could discover concerning " Richard Potter, the Celebrated Ventriloquist," and they were published in the *Granite Monthly* (Dover), II. 56.

where he died ; and yet there are scores of men still living who knew him intimately and one distinguished member of the New Hampshire bar now living pleaded causes at law before him.*

It may safely be affirmed that tradition is not very faithful to preserve facts, and not trustworthy when she assumes to do so. We are perhaps content to receive as history the traditions of the ancient peoples, preserved in the productions of an epic age, and to consider them, if not facts, as being better than facts. We give up with tardiness and reluctance the story of Poccahontas, and the Norse origin of the Old Wind Mill. But we are also aware that, in writing history, we place little reliance on traditions that are not strongly corroborative of each other, and coincident with every reasonable expectation.

And yet, I would not exclude tradition from among the original sources of history. Nor am I unaware that many things are stated as true, even in written history, on no more absolute authority than that concurrent circumstances indicate that they ought to be true.

Having therefore given this rapid survey of the

* This was Jerahmeel Bowers, sometime a merchant in New Chester, afterwards a resident of Bristol, where he was a magistrate from 1815 to 1842, and for some years held a justice-court almost every Saturday. The records of this court, in his own hand, comprised in three volumes, are in the archives of the New Hampshire Antiquarian Society. He had the head and body of a large man, but the lower limbs of a child, said to be not over a foot in length. He taught school many years, and was commonly known as "Master Bowers." Judge Nesmith told me he had tried several cases at law before him. Certain ascertained facts indicate that he was born in Franklin. He removed from Bristol to Bridgewater, but it is thought he died and was buried in Hebron. He left several children.

need and use of authentic information, and the growing importance, in the estimation of those best
acquainted with the subject, of all records of facts,
and all clews which lead to their discovery, I will
enumerate some of the most common, least prized,
and therefore most liable to be destroyed, among the
original sources of historical knowledge.

And passing over tradition, to which I have already
referred, and which, although to be used with great
caution, is by no means to be ignored, I will name

1. THE RELICS OF AN OBSOLETE PAST.

Recent as is the beginning of our history, yet there
are some things, besides Pine Tree Shillings and
Colonial Bills of Credit, once in common use in New
England, of which the "oldest inhabitant" has no
recollection. I remember that the venerable State
Historian, Dr. Bouton, searched a considerable time,
and no man's memory was able to afford him any
help, before he could discover the use of that
military accoutrement the "tumpline," so well known
to the Revolutionary soldier. *

Of the pre-historic age of Europe we know only
so much of the perished race as we are able to gather
from their implements, structures and remains, found
in the drift, in the caves and in the lakes. But from
these scanty sources of information, and from the de-
tached facts discovered in times and places far
apart, has been pieced together a tolerable knowledge of their physical characteristics, employments
and manner of life.†

* See N. H. Provincial Papers, vii. 591.

† In America the Stone Age of the aborigines was interrupted
and abolished, before passing to any higher attainment, by the in-
troduction of European methods.   The natives made haste to sup-

Now it is probably true that, of the implements and utensils ever in common use in New England, not only do some examples remain, but some knowledge of their purpose is retained by record or tradition. Of most of them the eldest portion of our people, and many of middle age, have a vivid recollection. But the children are growing up—yea, many are already themselves parents—who have no knowledge whatever, except as they have read or heard, of a great number of domestic implements once deemed

ply themselves with the more effective implements of the invaders, which were suited to their simple modes of life, and speedily abandoned their own rude constructions. In Mexico and Peru, the Spanish conquest arrested and destroyed a native American civilization remarkable for its character and achievements. If it ever had any "Stone Age," it had passed it long before, and had attained to the manufacture and use of bronze implements, ceramic wares, textile fabrics, and the working of the precious metals. Public records were kept in a rude picture-writing, on perishable materials, of which some fragments were preserved, and translations made by Spanish scholars. Hence it would be difficult to determine, at this distant day, how much of our knowledge of the native American races was derived from actual intercourse with them, and acquaintance with their methods by the settlers and conquerors of the country; and how much from archæological investigation. It is probable also that, in our reconstruction of the methods and characteristics of the Mound Builders, much vividness has been lent to our conceptions, by our knowledge of the ways and means of the Mexicans and Peruvians, derived from more authentic sources, with whom they appear to have been cognate, and of whom they may have been the ancestors. Nevertheless, it is certain that, had all knowledge of these remarkable American peoples, obtained by their conquerors, perished with them, an understanding, both accurate and extensive, of their physical traits, their modes of life, their form of government, their attainments in the arts, their knowledge of the physical sciences, and their methods of public administration, could have been derived solely from the study of their remains.

indispensable in a well-furnished New England household. And this is true, not only of the appliances for the internal economy of the home, but of those used in agriculture and mechanics; while, of those which remain, the form and fashion have been so changed, by modern inventions and improvements, that no true idea of the rude and durable character of those in use a hundred years ago can be obtained from them.

So completely have the methods of our industries and the manners of our domestic life changed within this present century, that 1800 and 1876 are, as compared with other ages of the world, hundreds of years apart. Nor can any written description, aided by the engraver's art, convey to the mind that vivid and accurate conception, of the discarded machinery of the past, that can be obtained from an examination of the things themselves. Hence it is safe to assume that the collections, classification and intelligent description of the implements and contrivances of an obsolete past in New England will not, probably,· at the end of another hundred years, be deemed a useless service to history. *

* During the greater part of nine months from Oct. 1876, I was engaged in literary labor at the Museum of the Antiquarian Society at Contoocook. This is located in the midst of a rural and mostly permanent population, where "old fashioned things" would be used many years after they had disappeared from cities, would be longest kept after they had been superceded by others, and hence the knowledge of their forms and uses longest retained. Nevertheless, I was constantly surprised by the enquiries of persons, twenty-five or thirty years of age and under, as to the names and uses of many articles, once as familiar in every home as spoons and platters; and, when told, they would generally say " they had heard the old folks tell of such things, but never saw one before." I had never before realized into how remote obscurity the recent past of New England had retreated.

2 SEPULCHRAL INSCRIPTIONS.

Our state is not yet so old that the sepulchral records of an early age are much decayed. But no one can visit the Burying Hill at Plymouth, or even the first cemeteries in Exeter and Haverhill (Ms.), without foreseeing how near at hand is the time when many of the tablets, bearing the record of the exit, age and family connection of our early settlers, will have ceased to exhibit any legible inscription. The old Dummerston slate, and the old gray sandstone, were very perishable materials for sepulchral monuments. Even inscriptions upon our enduring granite will yield their sharp-cut edges to the erosion of the elements, and become illegible after one or two hundred years. It does not preserve the facts committed to it like the syenite of Egypt.

It is possible, of course, that all facts thus inscribed on sepulchral stones are preserved in local records. But it is morally certain they are not, and it is doubly certain that no such completeness is found in the public records of the present day. I have it on the authority of the late Secretary of State [Gov. Prescott], that not above two-thirds, and probably not above one-half, of the deaths occurring in the state, are any year reported to his office ; and I know towns in which I think there has not been a birth or death recorded for fifteen years. A file of any one of the leading newspapers is probably a better record of deaths than our state elsewhere affords.

But, without reference to those of more modern date, it seems certain that any plan by which all sepulchral inscriptions made previous to the close of the first quarter of this century, at which time by far the larger part of those who fought in the war for independence had passed away, could be collected and indexed, would furnish the historian with innumerable and valuable facts scarcely obtainable in any other way.*

3 PRIVATE PAPERS.

Such as bonds, contracts, indentures, inventories, store- and shop-books, wills, deeds and private letters. Of the great mass of material of this kind, only a small part would be of any value. Most of it will and ought to be destroyed. But of such as remains to the third and fourth generation, and particularly of such as belonged or related to the early settlers of towns, a judicious and serviceable use could be made. It was from a document of this kind that the

---

* Since the publication of President Alden's admirable Collection of American Epitaphs in 1814, considerable attention has been paid to the subject of sepulchral records. It has been chiefly directed however to the transcription of such inscriptions as marked the resting-place of those who had achieved some distinction. Hence of slight value to the historian or genealogist, the facts being obtainable elsewhere. A few entire collections from old Cemeteries in Massachusetts have been printed. The Worcester *Society of Antiquity,* makes a specialty of this kind of effort, and published, with biographical notes, the Inscriptions from the Old Cemetery in that city, before the bodies were removed in 1878. The New Hampshire *Antiquarian Society* has a'so paid particular attention to the same subject, and has collected, and copied into its MS. Historical Collections, vols. I—V, and carefully indexed, the entire lists of inscriptions in the towns of Alexandria, Ashland, Bristol, Hanover, Hill, Hopkinton, and Trinity Church Yard, New York City. Also partial collections from Exeter, Franklin and Henniker, (N. H.) ; Barre, Calais, Montpelier and East Montpelier (Vt.) ; Greenwich, Haverhill, Hubbardston and Malden, (Ms.) ; Windsor (Ct.) ; and Mount Ida, Troy, N. Y. It has also in process of collection the entire lists of Canaan, Concord, Danbury, Dunbarton and Henniker.·

historic error concerning David Thomson's connection with Mason's schemes of colonization in New
Hampshire, above referred to, was corrected.

4 PRIVATE PAPERS ON PUBLIC AFFAIRS.

Of the importance of this class of documents much
might be said. The experienced antiquary and historian knows well their value. They are not formal
records, but supply much valuable information for
which records would be searched in vain. They
give the inside of affairs, of which records, if kept
and preserved, commonly give but the outside, or
no more than the frame-work. What a flood of
light is thrown on the drawing-rooms and social life,
on political intrigue and the interior of British administration, by the Diary of Samuel Pepys. Where
shall we look in the journals of the Parliament, or the
records of Westminster Hall, for that illustration of
the profligacy of the Court, which virtuous, old John
Evelyn gives in his private memoranda, when he
went to pay his respects to his Sovereign on that
Sunday night before Charles II. died? Even the
brilliant imagination of Macauley would have failed
to give such graphic descriptions of the men and
events of that time, had these two private documents
on public affairs been suppressed or destroyed.

An examination of Lossing's Field Books will
show how important is this class of documents as
sources of historical knowledge : and all history may
be said to have received its most vivid tints chiefly
from this kind of material.

Not only are great masses of matter, written to
town committees and selectmen by their agents and
representatives in the stormy days of the Indian wars,

and of the Revolution, stowed away in town, county and state offices, their contents and existence unknown, but, after all the vandalism of the paper-makers in the last seventeen years, there still remain valuable collections in private hands. They seemed of no importance at the time they were produced. Their real value is not generally understood by the parties into whose hands they have fallen. But they are often found to contain facts nowhere else recorded, and have sometimes given a new phase to history.

Similar to these are the records and transactions of informal gatherings, of a semi-public character. Assemblies of the people, self-constituted and unknown to the law, in which citizens discuss and deliberate upon public affairs, are germane to the genius of our republican institutions. In the crises and emergencies of our history, such gatherings have been frequent and influential. Such were the advisory bodies known as County Congresses, in the days of the revolution. Such were the conventions held in Dracut and Springfield, Mass., to devise means to regulate the price of commodities, and check the rapacity of merchants and speculators, in 1776.* Such was the Hartford Convention of 1814, whose records, remaining in private hands, were afterward edited and published by the secretary.† Such were the War Meetings of 1861, and the Loyalist Convention of Philadelphia in 1864. In modern times, the doings of such bodies, of any importance, become at once public through the columns of the newspa-

* See 2 Coll. N. H. Hist. Soc. 58 ; 8 N. H. State Papers, 628.

† History of the Hartford Convention : with a Review of the Policy of the United States Government which led to the War of 1812. By Theodore Dwight, Secretary of the Convention. 8°, pp. 447, New York and Boston, 1833.

per.   But it was not so anciently, and there can be
no doubt that much matter valuable to the local historian, has been irrecoverably lost.   Even of the first
two Provincial Congresses at Exeter, no list of the
members can be found, although these bodies cleared
the way for the foundations of a state government.
The records of our Hillsborough County Congresses always have been and are now in private hands,
and their discovery, after a long search, was purely
accidental, the parties to whom they had descended
having no knowledge of what they were, nor to what
they related.*

The controversy between Vermont and Connect-
icut, as to the honor of originating the measures
which resulted in the capture of Ticonderoga, 1775.
is thought to have been decided by a private letter
on public affairs.†

5 FAMILY RECORDS.

It is to be remembered and regretted, that this is
a subject almost wholly neglected in our day.   Every
student of history knows it is easier to discover the
records of families whose members have been dead
a hundred years, than of those born within the last
fifty.   He has also found that many men, of average
intelligence, do not know the names of their own
grandfathers ; and many who have *this* surprising
amount of genealogical information, know nothing

* They were discovered stowed away in a band-box, in the attic
of an ancient house in Amherst, by Edward D. Boylston, Esq.,
Editor of the *Farmers' Cabinet*, to whom they were readily given
up, and who has since had them in charge.   The publication of a
portion of them, by the State Historian (7 Prov. Papers, 447),
has placed so much of their contents beyond the possibility of loss.

† See Address of Hon. Lucius E. Chittenden before the Vt. Historical Society, at Ticonderoga, N. Y., 18 June, 1872, published
in the *Proceedings* of that year.

further about their ancestry, except their descent from one of the "three brothers who came over."

Judged by his utter neglect to make any family record, private or public ; his general reluctance to furnish any such information when requested—unless stimulated by a suspicion that it squints toward unclaimed estates in England, popularly supposed to be lying waste and disconsolate for want of American heirs to claim them—and the utter oblivion which possesses his intellect as to any ancestry whose existence he cannot recollect ; would lead to the conclusion that the average American cared little, either for his ancestors or his posterity.

Of the records of towns, of courts of probate and of law, of the military and the registry of deeds, all of which are required to be kept by law—all most important sources of historical knowledge—I shall say nothing. But of another class, closely allied to town records, and sometimes as important for historical purposes, and of which there is great neglect and waste, I desire to say something : *namely,*

6. THE RECORDS OF CHURCHES, PARISHES, PRECINCTS, VOLUNTARY ASSOCIATIONS, LITERARY AND OTHER SOCIETIES, INSTITUTIONS OF LEARNING, BENEVOLENT ORDERS, FINANCIAL AND COMMERCIAL CORPORATIONS.

Churches are important factors in determining the character of the local community. Their records often go back to the first settlement of the town, and contain items of information nowhere else to be found. These churches, by the subsequent shifting of population, become in many cases extinct. The records remain in private hands. Eventually they

are lost, unless recovered and preserved by responsible persons or societies. From our institutions of
learning have emanated potent influences, that have
greatly modified, not only the character of the communities where they were located, but have contrib-
uted to raise the average of culture in the state. —
Many of these, once famous and prosperous, have
become inoperative or extinct. Their records commonly remain in the hands of the last man who acts
as clerk of the corporation. They would throw
gleams of light on the history of many towns and lives,
distinguished for usefulness and power. Undoubted-
ly many other sources of historical knowledge could
be named, but these observations were intended to
be suggestive rather than exhaustive. What then
can be done, more than is being done, to preserve
the things which remain that are ready to perish?

Doubtless many plans might be suggested in answer to this question. I take the liberty therefore to
set forth certain things which appear to me reasonable and practicable, if undertaken by a sufficient
number, of the right kind of men, and pursued with
systematic, co-operative endeavor.

1.   I would like to see a periodical, after the style
of *Farmer and Moore's Collections*, or the *New England Historical and Genealogical Register*, established
and supported in every State ; devoted mainly to the
history and biography of that state, or whatever
throws light upon it ; to include monthly lists of marriages and deaths ; and obituaries of prominent natives and residents of the state.   Such a periodical,
if published under the auspices of a responsible Society, or conducted by a judicious and trusted man,
would deserve to be sustained.

2. A systematic and continued endeavor, by Historical and Antiquarian Societies, to collect, classify
label, index, and render as available as possible, all
such records and manuscripts as I have referred to
and others of equal value. To have all the most
important carefully copied into volumes, and memoranda of the contents of all others of sufficient importance to be preserved legibly engrossed therein ;
and the names of places and persons alphabetically
indexed. The same to be a part of the stated work of
the Society. That such documents as were discovered worthy of the labor, the permanent possession of
which could not be obtained, including papers owned
by other states or societies (relating to the state in
which the particular society is located), be copied in
the same manner where permission could be obtained, and so much as possible of this matter, floating
about in private hands and every year running to
waste, be saved and rendered available for the historian's use.*

* To show that this plan is not altogether chimerical I will say,
that it was made a part of the permanent work of the New Hampshire Antiquarian Society at the time of its organization in 1873,
and has thus far been systematically pursued. The Manuscripts
are copied into Demy-Folio volumes, of the size commonly used in
Registers' offices, by a Historical Committee of seven appointed
each year, and one volume, thoroughly and completely indexed,
commonly constitutes the work of this committee for one year.
The IXth is now (1879) in preparation. Their contents, consist-
ing wholly of original matter, would fill twelve volumes of 500
pages each the size of this. After the completion of the IVth
volume they were examined carefully for the greater part of two
days by the State Historian, the late Rev. Nathaniel Bouton, D.D.,
who, in an address to the Annual Meeting in 1877 spoke of the accuracy and thoroughness of the work in terms more emphatic than
I feel at liberty to quote, and declared this part of the Society's

3. To see the Legislature of each state provide by
law for the collection, classification and preservation
of public records ; either (1) in accordance with a re-
commendation of Gov. Prescott, to the legislature
of New Hampshire in 1877 ; * or, (2) by the erec-
tion of a State Department of History, or of Public
Records, providing suitable accommodations, the
same as it now provides for the archives of the State,
in which should be gathered either copies or originals
of the ancient records of towns, the records of the
proprietors of towns previous to their incorporation,
many of which are still in private hands, and all other
records and documents of historical value that could
be secured.   In connection with this, the creation of
a permanent office of State Historian, or Keeper of
Public Records, with suitable assistance, whose duty
it should be to look after, and endeavor to secure
for the state, such various documents as I have herein-
before named, or some of them, and to place all such
records and documents, as fast as collected, in the

labor, if pursued in the manner in which it had been commenced,
" an invaluable service to history."   For full account of the manner of conducting this labor, see *Granite Monthly*, I. 154.

* I recommend the passage of an act making the register of deeds
in each county the custodian of the papers not required for the im-
mediate use of the town. With slight expense, under the direction of the county commissioners, alcoves could be constructed in
the fire proof vaults in the register's office, equal to the number of
towns in the county. The town-clerks, under the direction of the
selectmen, should be required to deposit such papers in these vaults,
properly folded, filed, and labelled. The advantage to the public
from such a change would be incalculable. All ancient and important papers would then be as sacredly preserved as the title
deeds to real estate in the same towns.   —*Gov. Prescott to the
Legislature of New Hampshire, 1877.*

in the best possible condition for consultation, and furnish copies when desired for a fixed fee. That means should be provided by law for making this the depository of all municipal records (either by copies or originals) up to some given date, say 1825, with provision for their augmentation to within fifty years, every quarter of a century. I cannot help believing that such an arrangement would be found more convenient, and more acceptable to those who would have most frequent occasion to use them, either for purposes of history or law, than any which divided and dispersed them in smaller collections ; and much more so than their present scattered, disordered and dilapidated condition. This latter is only an outline of something that seems desirable.

Of course I know the general constitution of the legislative body, and hence how Utopian any such scheme would seem to be. But it is safe to assume in the light of experience, that whatever shall be thought desirable by the " wise men " of any given state, for the better keeping and more facile use of the local and general public records, the people of that state can be educated to demand and the legislature to grant. It is true I " have a zeal " on this subject ; but I trust it is somewhat "according to knowledge." Long experience in searching the fields of local history has taught me how important sometimes are papers regarded as worthless by their possessors ; how easily dates and circumstances needed to complete the history of a life or place are neglected and lost; in what a confused, deplorable and perishing condition are the proprietary and early records of towns, and particularly the loose and unrecorded town papers. The various Historical and

Antiquarian Societies have rendered invaluable service, of the kinds and in the directions indicated
above, however little their work is appreciated by the
masses. Nevertheless, there are some lines of re-
search and some fields of enterprise not yet very
thoroughly explored, much less are they occupied
and cultivated, which promise rich returns and abund-
ant harvests to the industrious antiquary ; and it has
appeared to me that so favorable a time will never re-
cur for the successful gathering-up of the fragments
which remain, for securing and preserving many
relics and records of an obsolete past—a phase of
New England life which can have no repetition in the
centuries to come—as does occur to us of this generation.   And if to the endeavors of those gentlemen
who, appreciating the value and importance of such
sources of historical knowledge, have acquired facili-
ty and skill in their arrangement and use, the State
would supply the sanction of law and the sinews of
war for a thorough and systematic campaign, and for
the future care of the spoils, it would perform an act
for the promotion of the public honor and the public
good, for which after generations, benefitted by her
provident foresight, would rise up and call her blessed.

NOTE.—Since the foregoing pages were printed, I have been
gratified to learn that the New Hampshire Historical Society had
appointed a committee of eminent gentlemen to devise and
recommend means for the better preservation of municipal records and papers.